MINISTRY OF MUNITIONS

Technical Department— Aircraft Production.

▽ ▽
▽

I.C. 619.

Kingsway,

W.C.2.

REPORT ON THE
FRIEDRICHSHAFEN BOMBER.

MARCH, 1918.

J. G. WEIR,
Lieut. Colonel,
Controller, Technical Department.

The Naval & Military Press Ltd

Published by

The Naval & Military Press Ltd
Unit 10 Ridgewood Industrial Park,
Uckfield, East Sussex,
TN22 5QE England

Tel: +44 (0) 1825 749494
Fax: +44 (0) 1825 765701

www.naval-military-press.com
www.military-genealogy.com

in association with

Imperial War Museums
iwm.org.uk

MINISTRY OF MUNITIONS

Technical Department— Aircraft Production.

▽ ▽
▽

I.C. 619.

KINGSWAY,

W.C.2.

REPORT ON THE
FRIEDRICHSHAFEN BOMBER.

MARCH, 1918.

J. G. WEIR,
Lieut.-Colonel,
Controller, Technical Department.

T.5. D.802/338. 21/6/18.

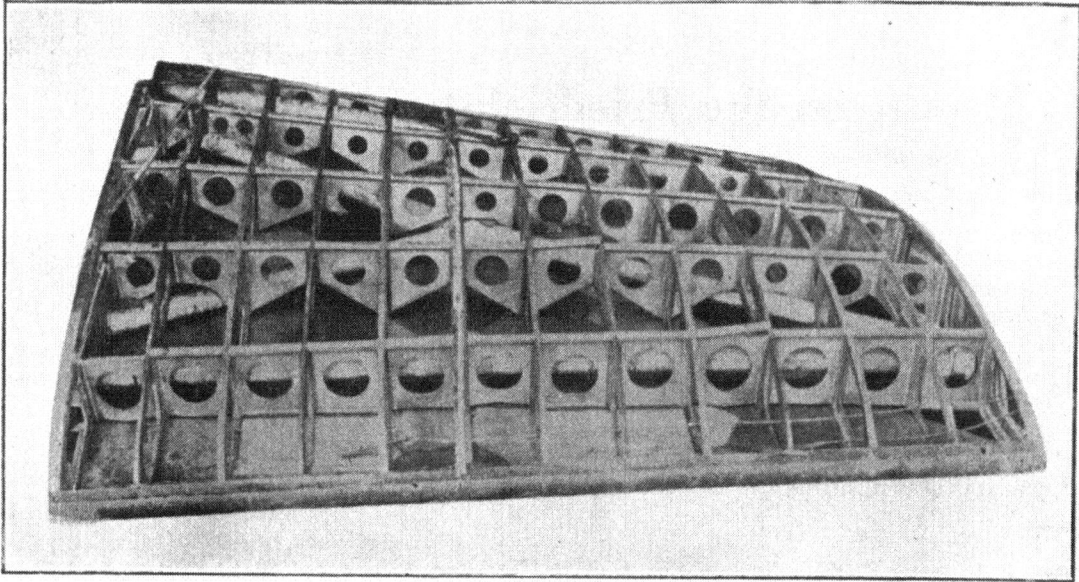

FIG. 1. CENTRE SECTION OF LOWER MAIN PLANE WITH THREE-PLY
SURFACING REMOVED.

FIG. 20. VIEW LOOKING DOWN THE INSIDE OF THE FUSELAGE
FROM THE MAIN NACELLE, SHOWING TRAP-DOOR AND
AFTER-GUNNER'S FOLDING SEAT.

1

Report on the Friedrichshafen Bomber.

This machine, which bears the mark F.D.H. G.3. 326/17, was brought down by anti-aircraft fire at Isbergues on the night of the 16th February. A shell made a direct hit on the right-hand engine at a height of 8,000 to 9,000 feet, after which the machine covered about six miles and made a fairly good landing.

Various parts of the structure bear different dates, that on the tail being 14/1/18. The main spars are branded with a small crown and the letters Z.A.K. The following is painted on the side of the body:—

Leergewicht (weight empty), 2,695 kilogrammes=5,929 lbs.
Nutzlast (useful load), 1,235 kilogrammes=2,717 lbs.
Zulassiges Gesamtgewicht (permissible total weight), 3,930 kilogrammes=8,646 lbs.

CREW.

This machine carried its full complement of four persons, namely, pilot, fore-gunner, after-gunner, and bomber. It is known, however, that the number of crew varies considerably, as some machines of this type have only carried two persons. The accommodation is so arranged that the personnel can easily change places, all the cockpits being intercommunicating.

GENERAL DESCRIPTION.

The general design of the machine is shown in the attached drawing, which gives plan and front and side elevations.

The principal dimensions are as follows:—

Span	78 ft.
Maximum chord	7 ft. 8 in.
Gap	7 ft.
Dihedral angle in the vertical plane	$1\frac{1}{2}°$
Dihedral angle in the horizontal plane	6°
Total area of main planes	934.4 sq. ft.
Area of upper main planes without flap	480 ,,
Area of lower main planes without flap	454.4 ,,
Load per square foot	9.24 lbs
Weight per horse power	16.6 lbs.
Area of flap of upper wing	21.6 sq. ft.
Balance area	1.8 ,,
Area of flap on lower wing	16 ,,
Balance area	1.56 ,,
Total area of fixed tail planes	57.6 ,,
Total area of elevators	32 ,,
Balance area of one elevator	1.7 ,,
Area of fin	20 ,,
Area of rudder	19.2 ,,
Balance area of rudder	8 ,,
Maximum cross section of body	19.2 ,,
Horizontal area of body	133 ,,
Vertical area of body	131.2 ,,
Length overall	42 ft.

The machine is built up upon a central section, to which are attached the forward and rearward portions of the fuselage and the main planes. This central section comprises the main cell or cabin of the body, containing the tanks, bombs, etc. It also embraces the engines and the central portion of the upper and lower planes. The latter, together with the engine struts, are largely built up of steel tube, as is also the landing gear.

The central portion of the body, which measures 4' across by 4' 3" in height, consists of a box formation made of ply wood, strengthened by longerons and diagonals, and transversely stiffened by ply-wood bulkheads. The bulkhead furthest forward acts as an instrument board, behind which are side by side the seats of the pilot and his assistant. The former has a fixed upholstered seat. whilst that of the latter is folding, consisting of a light steel tubular framework with a webbing back-rest.

Underneath these two seats is the lower main petrol tank. Behind this cockpit the body is roofed in with ply wood, the rear part of which roofing is detachable so as to give access to the second main petrol tank, which is at the rear end of the main body section. By this means a small cabin or covered passage-way is provided, at each side of which are the racks for the smaller bombs.

CENTRAL PORTION OF WINGS.

The central and non-detachable portion of the upper plane has a span of 19′ 5″, whilst at each side of the nacelle the lower plane fixed portion measures 7′ 8″. The main wing spars in this central portion are of steel tube, roughly 2″ in diameter, with a wall thickness of ⅒″.

As shown in the photograph Fig. No. 1, these spars are braced by steel tubes arranged in the form of an X, the manner in which the bracing tubes are attached to the main spars being shown in the sketch Fig. 2.

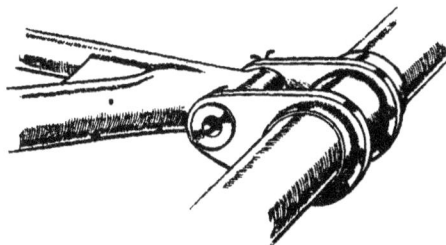

FIG. 2.

The lugs are built up by welding, and are pinned and rivetted in position, the joint being of the plain knuckle type.

The upper surface of the lower plane is, so far as the central section is concerned, covered in with three-ply wood.

In this portion the main ribs are of three-ply, with spruce flanges. Between each main rib is a cut-away rib, the design of which is shown in the sketch Fig. 3. This, unlike the main ribs, is one piece of wood, and not built up. For the greater part of its length it applies to the top surface only, being cut away to pass clear of the cross bracing tubes.

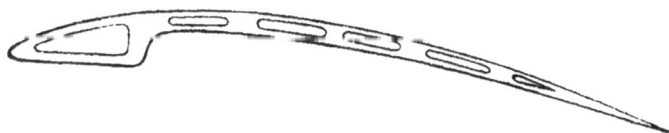

FIG. 3.

FIG. 4.　　FIG. 5.

As shown in the photograph Fig. 1, the plane is further stiffened with transverse members consisting of three-ply panels between each rib strengthened by grooved pieces top and bottom. The latter are attached as shown in the sketch Fig. 4, and the attachment of the flanges of the main ribs is shown in Fig. 5.

The central section of the upper main plane is in one piece and is covered top and bottom with fabric. In order to facilitate the removal of the engines, detachable panels measuring 1′ 11½″ long by 1′ 8″ deep are let into the trailing edge immediately over the engine bearers. These panels are socketted in front, and at the rear are joined up at the trailing edge with U section sheet steel clips and bolts.

The struts which connect the top of the nacelle to the upper plane are tubular and of stream-line section, as are also the engine bearer struts. A section of one of the latter is given in Fig. 6. The thickness of the wall is one-sixteenth of an inch.

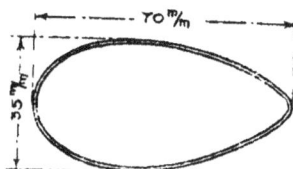

FIG. 6.

3

The method of attaching the lower end of the engine struts to the tubular steel spars is shown in the sketch Fig. 7, from which it will be seen that a welded Y socket is used and secured by a pin joint, the ends of the pin acting as anchorages for the attachment of the bracing wires.

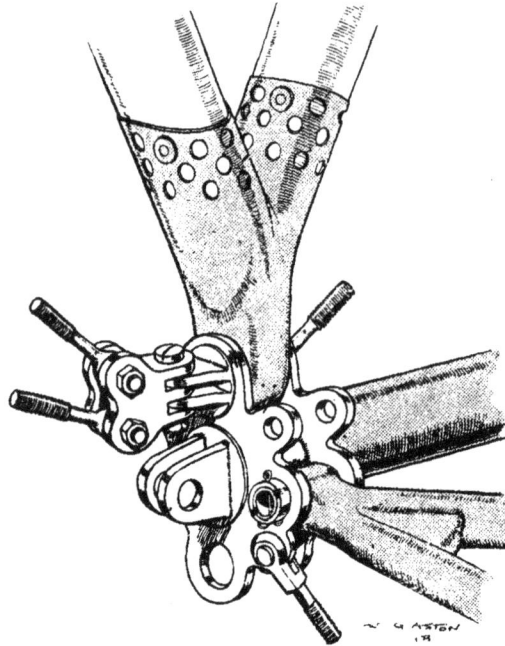

FIG. 7.

This sketch also shows the lugs which respectively support the detachable portion of the main planes and the vertical strut of the landing chassis. The engine bearer struts are pushed into the Y socket and pinned in position, the pins being afterwards brazed into the socket. At their upper ends the engine struts are fixed to the top plane spars with pin joints, as shown in Figs. 8 and 9, the attachment differing according to the number of wire bracings that are to be taken to each joint.

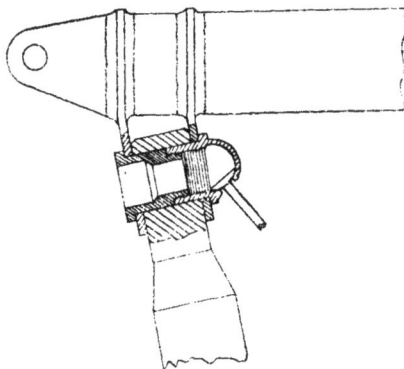

FIG. 8.

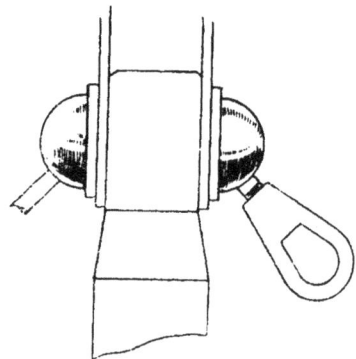

FIG. 9.

CONSTRUCTION OF WINGS.

The detachable portions of the wings are fixed to the centre section by pin joints, one part of which is shown in Fig. 7, the male portion being represented in Fig. 10. The chord of the wing in the line of flight varies from approximately 7' 8" to 7' 5", and the wing section is shown shaded in Fig. 11. In order to provide a basis of comparison the R.A.F. 14 wing section is superimposed and drawn to the same scale.

4

FIG. 10.

The main spars are placed one metre apart, the front spar being 272 mms. in the rear of the leading edge. Both spars are of the built up box type, as shown in Figs. 12 and 13. The former is the leading spar and the latter the rear spar. These spars are of spruce, and each half is furnished with several splices, so that the greatest single length of timber in them is not more than 14'. The splices, which occur in each half alternately, are of the plain bevel type about 15" long and wrapped with fabric. A fabric wrapping is also applied at short intervals along the spar.

Internal cross bracing between the main spars is afforded by steel tube cross members and cables attached as shown in the sketch Fig. 10.

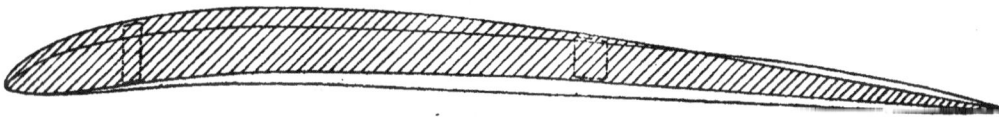

FIG. 11.

The main spar joint consists of a steel plate 19 mms. thick embedded in the spar end and held in position by 5 bolts, which pass through a strapping plate surrounding the end of the spar. This plate also carries the attachment for the bracing cable and is furnished with a spigot which locates the bracing tube. It will be seen that at this point the spar is provided with tapered packing pieces of hard wood glued and held in position by fabric wrapping.

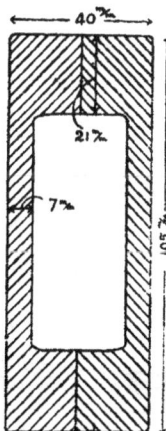

FIG. 12.

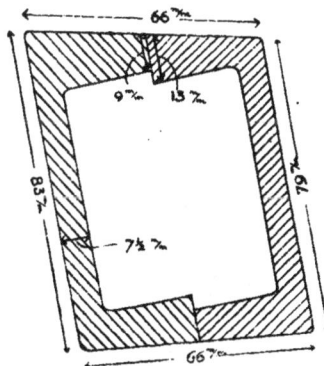

FIG. 13.

5

The main ribs are placed 360 mms. apart. Between them are auxiliary formers, consisting of strips of wood 20 mms.×10 mms. thick, which run from the leading edge to the rear spar. The main ribs consist of ply wood webs socketted into grooved spruce flanges, which are tapered off as shown in Fig. 5, except where they are met by a longitudinal stringer. The leading edge is solid wood moulded to a semi-circular section of approximately 65 mms. diameter. Where the rib web abuts against it, packing pieces are glued each side. Between the main spars the web of the rib is divided by three vertical strips into four panels and in each of these it is perforated, leaving an edge all round about 72 mms. wide.

As shown in Fig. 10, the upper flange of the main ribs is carried clear of the leading spar by means of packing pieces. In the case of the rear spar, packing pieces are also used under the rib flange, as shown in Fig. 14.

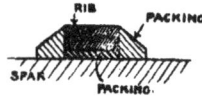

FIG. 14.

The lower main planes for a width of about 2′ 3″ at their inner end are covered as to their top surfaces with three-ply wood.

The interplane struts are attached to the main spars by joints of the type shown in Fig. 15 This, it will be seen, follows the typical German practice of partially universal jointed mountings for the cable attachments. At the points of attachment of these strut joints, suitably tapered packing pieces of hard wood surround the spars, which at these points are also wrapped with fabric.

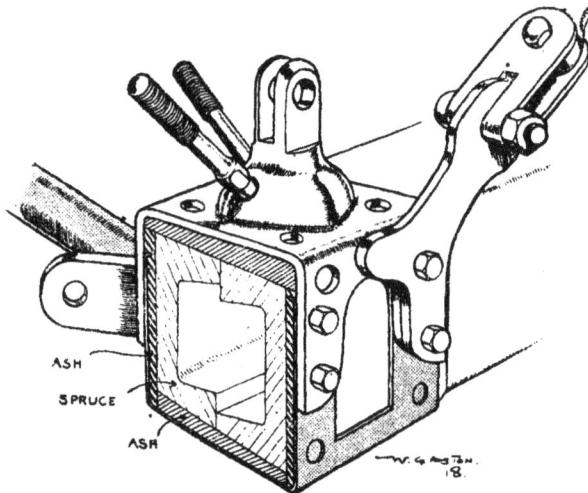

FIG. 15.

STRUTS.

Outside of the centre section the interplane struts are of wood built up, as shown in the section Fig. 16, of five separate pieces. The curved portions are of timber which has not yet been identified, but is apparently of poor quality. The cross web is of ash. The strut is wrapped at frequent intervals with strips of fabric and is fitted with a socket joint of the type shown in Fig. 17. The outer pair of struts are of smaller section than the main struts, but are built up in a similar manner. Their section is 125 mms.×40 mms.

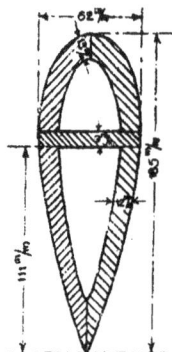

FIG. 16.

FIG. 17.

AILERONS.

The framework is principally of welded steel tube wrapped with fabric.

A notable point is the thick section of the leading edge of the balanced portion, as shown in Fig. 18.

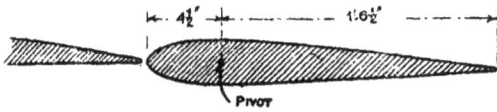

FIG. 18.

FIN AND FIXED TAIL-PLANES.

The framework of these is steel tube and in the case of the tail-planes wooden stringers running fore and aft are arranged at intervals. The tail-planes are supported by diagonal steel tubes of streamline section, on the under side of which sharp steel points are welded to prevent these stays being used for lifting purposes.

ELEVATORS AND RUDDERS.

The framework in each case is of steel tube, the main tube being 35 mms. in diameter and the remainder 15 mms.

BRACING.

Throughout the wings, both internally and externally, the bracing is by means of multistrand steel cable.

FUSELAGE. *(Rear Portion.)*

At the after-gunner's cockpit the section of the fuselage has a rounded top, which is gradually smoothed down into flat. The section, for the greater part of the length, is rectangular, and the frame is built up in the usual manner with square section longerons and verticals, the joints being arranged as shown in Fig. 19. The cross bracing wires along the sides, top, bottom, and diagonal are of steel piano wire and are covered with strips of fabric, as shown in this sketch, where they lie adjacent to the fabric fuselage covering.

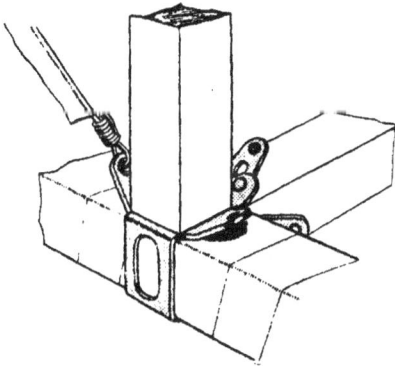

FIG. 19.

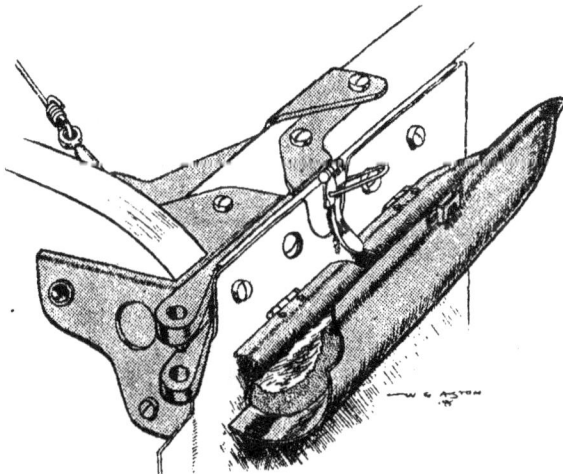

FIG. 21.

The vertical and horizontal compression members are located by spigots. The joint consists of a plate which completely surrounds the longerons, its two ends being rivetted together to form a diagonal bracing strip. For the last few feet at the tail the fuselage is covered with thin three-ply.

Fig. No. 20 is a view looking down the rear portion of the fuselage. The fuselage is covered with fabric, which is held in position by a lacing underneath and is consequently bodily removable.

The floor of the after-gunner's cockpit is elevated above the bottom of the fuselage. Immediately underneath this cockpit is a large trapdoor, shown in the photograph No. 20, and also by dotted lines in the plan view of the aeroplane. This is hinged at its rearward end and furnished with two large celluloid windows. It is held in its " up " position by a long spring and a snap clip. No means could be found by which it could be fixed in its closed position. As footsteps are provided for all the cockpits, this trapdoor is evidently not intended for ingress and egress. It could be employed in connection with a machine gun firing backwards, as in the Gotha, but no machine gun mounting was fixed in this machine for this purpose.

The rear portion of the fuselage is attached to the centre section of the body by a clip at each corner. This is shown in Fig. 21. The rear portion carries a male lug, shown in Fig. 49, which engages with the two eyes, and is held in position by a ⅜ths bolt. Four other bolts in tension pass through the sheet metal clip, as shown in the sketch. In each case the lugs are

7

FIG. 22. FRONT PORTION OF THE NACELLE.

FIG. 23. INSIDE OF THE FRONT COCKPIT.

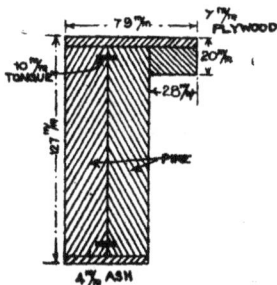

FIG. 24.

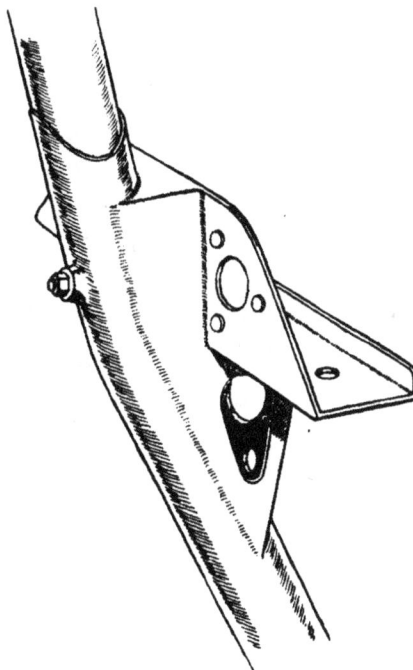

FIG. 25.

furnished with sheet steel extensions which, as shown in the sketch Fig. 21, are sunk flush into the top and bottom surfaces of the fuselage longerons and are there held with three bolts. The corner joint is welded sheet steel, and there is an additional diagonal sheet steel joint which serves the secondary purpose of providing an anchorage for the bracing wires.

As this fuselage joint is level with the plane of rotation of the propellers, it is armoured both on the nacelle and on the rear portion of the fuselage with a hinged covering of stout sheet steel lined with felt. A plate of armour a foot wide also extends down each side of the nacelle at this point.

FORWARD COCKPIT.

This is attached to the main body by four bolts with clips similar to those just described. It consists of a light wooden framework, covered throughout by three-ply. Two views of this portion of the machine are given in the photographs Figs. 22 and 23. This cockpit can be divided off from the main cockpit by means of a fabric curtain. Its occupant is provided with the folding seat, as shown, and manages a gun and the bomb dropping gear.

ENGINE MOUNTING.

The engine bearers have the section shown in Fig. 24, and are each built up of two pieces of pine united by tongues. On their top surface they are faced with ply wood and at the bottom with ash. A strip of ash applied to the upper outer corner of the bearer gives it an "L" section, and has screwed into it the threaded sockets for the set screws of the lower part of the engine fairing. The engine bearers taper sharply at each end. They are mounted on the "V" struts by means of acetylene welded brackets, constructed as shown in sketch, Fig. 25. These, it will be seen, are of box form, and form a liner round the streamline tube.

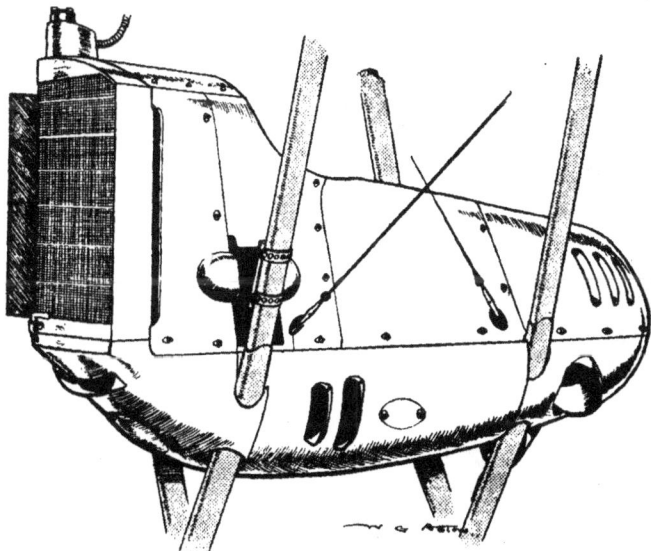

FIG. 26.

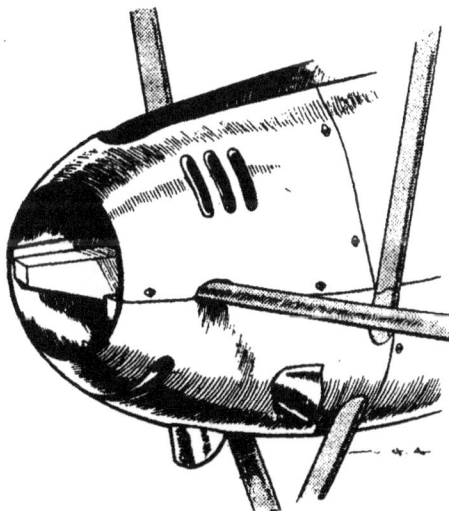

FIG. 27.

9

The engine cowling is a particularly fine piece of work, and two views are given in sketches 26 and 27. The lower portion is attached to the engine bearers by set screws, but the upper part is readily detachable, being furnished with turn buttons. This cowling allows the cylinders of the engine to be exposed to the air. A large scoop is placed in front, so as to permit a free flow of air over the bottom and sides of the crankchamber, whilst at the rear three large trumpet shaped cowls are provided so that a draught of air is forced against the crankcase in the neighbourhood of the carburetter air intake. In the rear the fairing abuts against the propeller nave, whilst in front it is attached to the radiator. It will be noticed that at each side of the radiator are narrow air scoops, the object of which is to promote a draught past the oil tank and front cylinder heads.

ENGINES.

The motors are the standard 260 H.P. Mercedes with six cylinders in line. Full details of this engine have been published, and it is only, therefore, necessary to notice one or two points in connection with the installation.

A new departure is the interconnection of the throttle and ignition advance controls. This is carried out in the manner illustrated diagrammatically in Fig. 28. It will be seen that a considerable movement of the throttle can be made independently of the ignition advance. In the Mercedes carburetter the throttle is so arranged that it cannot be fully opened near the ground with-

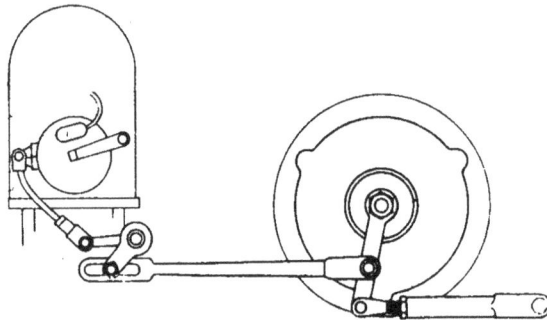

FIG. 28.

out providing too weak a mixture, and it is thought possible that the full ignition advance is not obtained until this critical opening is reached.

On several German bombing aeroplanes grease pumps for lubricating the water pump spindle have been found. Fig. 29 shows the design as fitted to the Friedrichshafen. It consists of a ratchet and pawl operated grease pump, secured by a bracket to one of the engine struts, and worked from the pilot's cockpit by a lever, and a stranded steel cable passing over a pulley, the pawl being returned by a long coiled spring.

The engine numbers are respectively MN.32299 and MN.36228.

Photograph Fig. 30 shows the exhaust pipe. This is of new design, although it incorporates the well-known expansion joints attached to the flanges. It will be seen that it is fitted with what amounts to a rudimentary silencer, whereas in previous machines of a similar type to the Friedrichshafen an open-ended exhaust pipe was used.

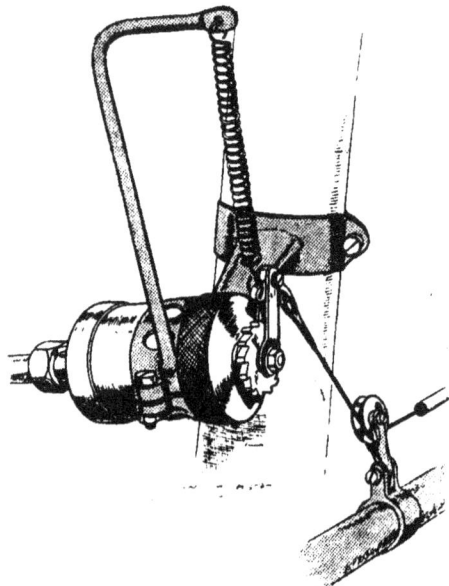

FIG. 29.

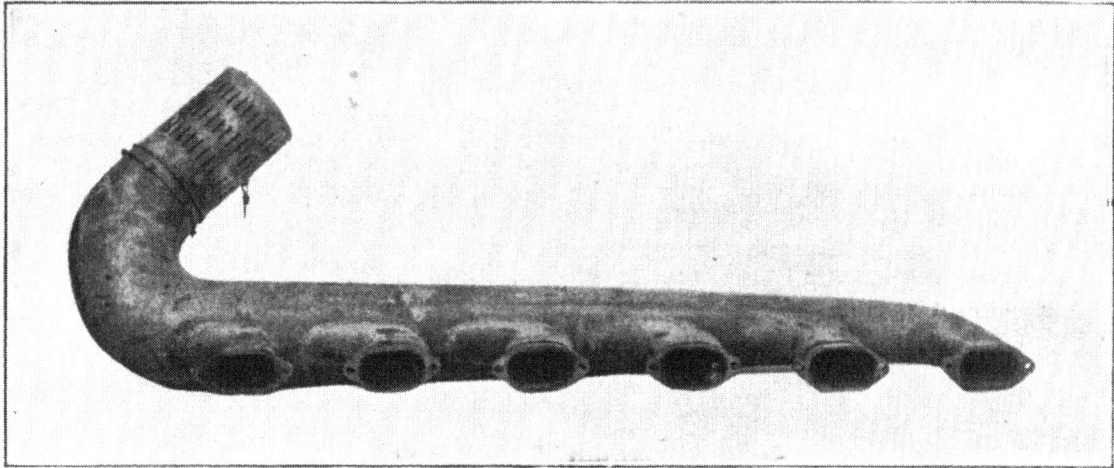

FIG. 30. THE EXHAUST PIPE OF THE 260 H.P. MERCEDES ENGINE.

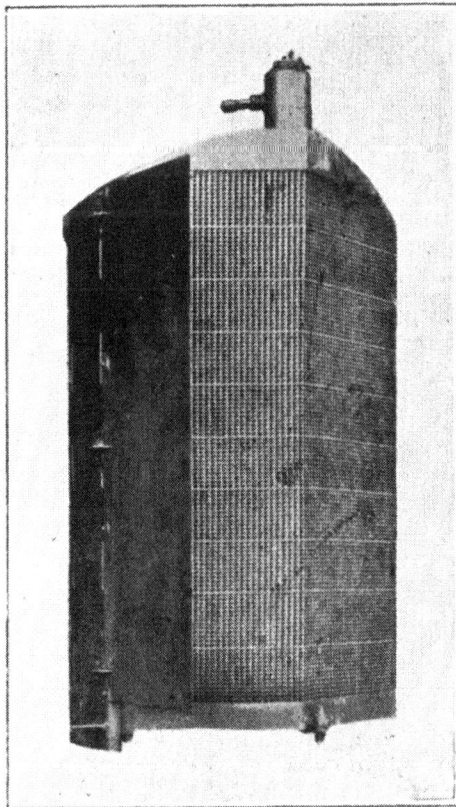

FIG. 33. RADIATOR, WITH SHUTTER OPEN.

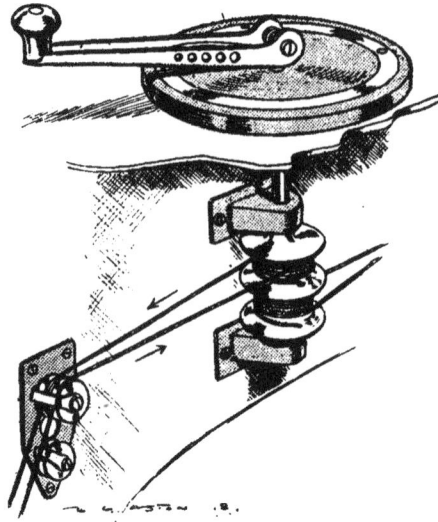

FIG. 31.

RADIATORS.

Each radiator is provided with an electric thermometer fitted into the water inlet pipe. as shown in sketch, Fig. 32, these thermometers being wired up to a dial on the dashboard, which is furnished with a switch, so that the temperature of either radiator can be taken independently.

Each radiator is provided with an electric thermometer fitted into the water inlet pipe, apparently square tubes to the number of 4,134, and measuring roughly 6 mms. each way. The radiator with shutter full open is shown in Fig. 33.

The honeycomb radiators are of "V" section, and each is provided with a shutter which covers up a little more than a third of the cooling surface. This shutter is fitted with a stop, so that when fully opened it lies in the line of flight of the aeroplane. It is opened or closed according to circumstances by the gear, shown in the sketch, Fig. 31, of which the handle is mounted on the roof of the nacelle, immediately behind the pilot's seat. Three positions are provided for the handle, which operates the two shutters simultaneously by means of return cables.

Immediately above the main radiator, and let into the upper main plane between the front spar and the leading edge, is a small auxiliary tank, illustrated in Fig. 34. This is furnished with a trumpet shaped vent in the direction of the line of flight, and is furnished with two outlets, one to the head of the main radiator, and the other to the water pump. The function of this tank is evidently to prevent the pump from priming.

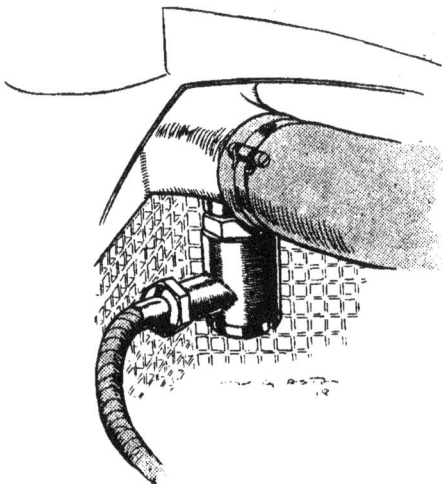

FIG. 32.

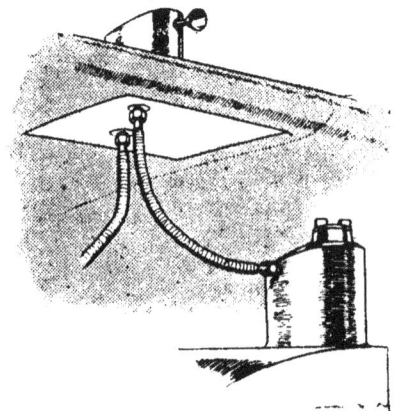

FIG. 34.

12

OIL PUMP.

The main supply of oil is carried in sumps forming part of the base chamber. A secondary supply of oil, from which a small fresh charge is drawn at every stroke of the oil pump, is contained in a cylindrical tank supported by brackets from the engine struts, and placed immediately behind the radiator. This tank is shown in photograph Fig. 35, and has a capacity of 25 litres=5½ gallons. Each tank is furnished with a glass level, which is visible from the pilot's seat.

PETROL TANKS.

The two main tanks which are placed, one under the pilot's seat and the other at the top rear end of the nacelle, contain 270 litres=59½ gallons each, and are made of brass. Each is provided with a Maximall level indicator, which employs the principle of a float operating a dial by means of a cable enclosed in a system of pipes.

A hand pump is fitted convenient to the pilot, and pressure is normally provided by the pumps installed in each engine. An auxiliary tank, holding approximately 13 gallons, is concealed in the upper main plane, not immediately over the nacelle but a little to the left side. This auxiliary tank is fitted with a level, as shown in Fig. 36, which is visible from the cockpit. The auxiliary tank appears to be used only for starting purposes. It is covered with a sheet of fabric held in position by "patent fasteners." A photograph is given in Fig 37.

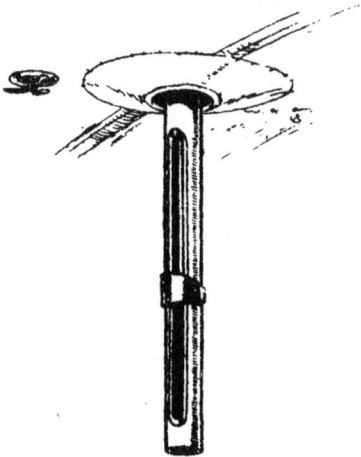

FIG. 36.

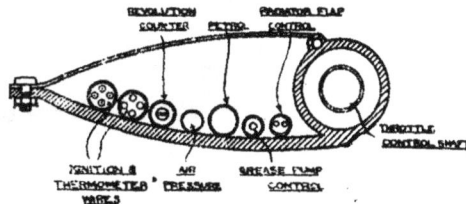

FIG. 38.

ENGINE CONTROLS.

Running from each engine to the nacelle is a horizontal streamline casing, containing the various engine controls. A section showing the arrangement of these inside the fairing is given in the sketch, Fig. 38. The leading edge of the streamline casing consists of a steel tube, to which are welded narrow steel strip brackets, to the rear end of which are bolted thinner strips which are hinged in front to the tube. The whole is then enclosed in a sheet aluminium fairing.

Through the leading tube passes the throttle control rod for each engine, the two throttles being worked either together or independently by the ratchet levers, shown in Fig. 39. These are mounted on a shelf convenient to the pilot's left hand. This control requires a con-

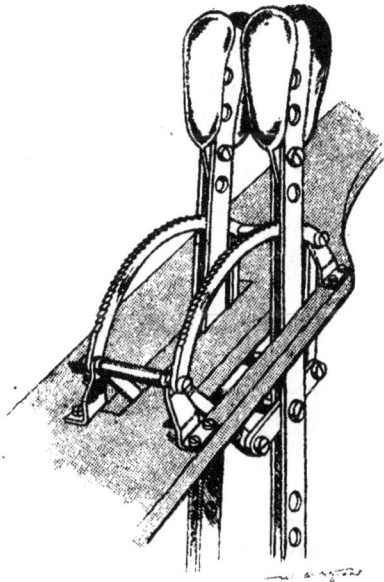

FIG. 39.

Fig. 35. Oil Tank. This is placed immediately behind the radiator.

Fig. 37. Gravity petrol tank let into the centre section of the upper plane. Its fabric cover is held down by press-buttons. Note the detachable panel in the trailing edge of the plane.

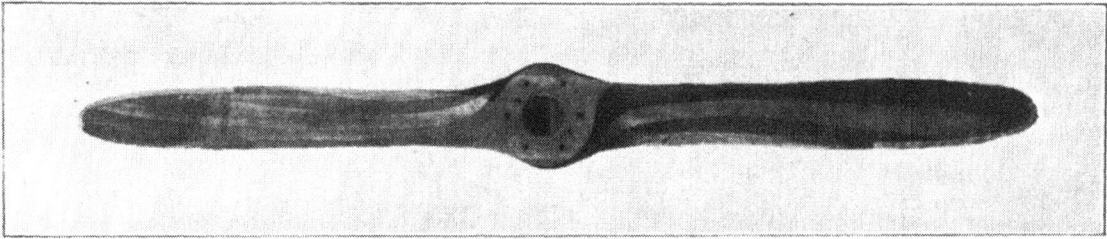

FIG. 40. FRONT VIEW OF THE PROPELLER. NOTE THE TWO ADDITIONAL BOLT HOLES.

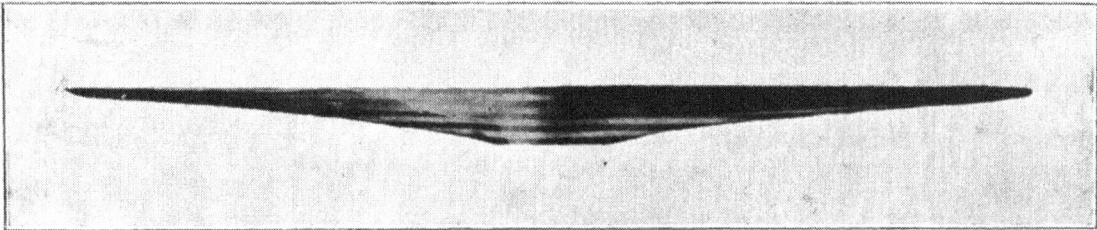

FIG. 41. SIDE VIEW OF THE PROPELLER.

FIG. 46. MAIN LANDING CHASSIS WITH FABRIC FAIRING REMOVED.

15

siderable number of bell cranks and countershafts, but was noticably free from backlash. The throttle is opened by the pilot pulling the levers towards him.

On the dashboard are two revolution counters and two air pressure indicators. The metal parts of these dials are painted red for the left engine and green for the right, and the same colouring applies to the magneto switches, one of which contains a master switch which applies to both magnetos on both engines.

PIPING.

The various systems of piping are distinguished by being painted different colours, thus the petrol pipes are white, arrows being also painted on them to show the direction of flow; air pressure pipes are blue, and pipes for cable controls grey.

PROPELLER.

The propellers are made by the Luckenwalde Propellerwerke, Niendorf. Each propeller is 3.08 metres in diameter and is made of nine laminations, which are alternately walnut and ash, except one which appears to be of maple. Photographs Figs. 40 and 41 show the propeller, which has the last 20 ins. of its blade edged with brass. The pitch is approximately 1.8 metres and the maximum width of the blade 220 millimetres.

CONTROLS.

Only one set of control gears is fitted, but as pointed out, the seating accommodation is so arranged that any of the crew can take charge if, and when, necessary.

The elevator and aileron control is shown in sketch Fig. 42. It consists of a tubular steel pillar mounted on a cranked cross bar at its foot. The ailerons are worked by cables passing over a drum on the wheel, whence they descend through fibre guides on the cross bar to another wheel mounted on a countershaft below, from which they are taken along inside the leading edge of the lower wing and finally over pulleys up to the aileron levers on the top plane. The latter are partially

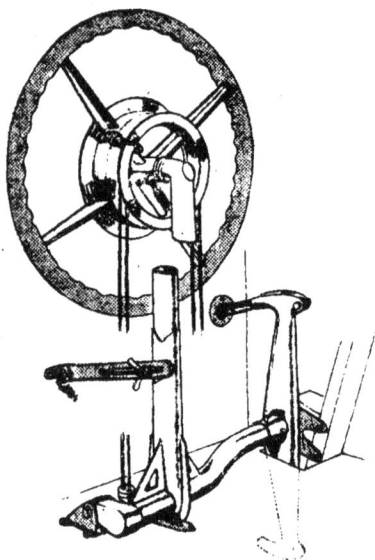

FIG. 42.

FIG. 43.

concealed in slots let into the trailing edge of the wing. The upper and lower ailerons are connected by means of pin jointed tubular steel struts of streamline section.

It will be observed from Fig. 42 that a locking device whereby the elevator control can be fixed in any desired position is fitted, and consists of a slotted link which can be clamped by a butterfly nut to the control lever. This link is hinged to a small bracket attached to the panel below the pilot's seat.

Fig. 43 shows the rudder control, from which cables are taken over pulleys and through housings in the nacelle and finally to the end of the fuselage. The cranked rudder bar is of light steel tube and is arranged to be placed in the pivot box in either of two positions. It is furnished with light steel tubular hoops which act as heel rests and are adjustable. A locking clip is fitted on the floor of the cockpit so that the rudder can be fixed in its neutral position.

A novel type of trimming gear is an interesting item of the control. Movement of the elevator control from the normal upright position of the stick is made against the tension of one of two springs which can be alternately extended and relaxed by means of a winch connected to them, as shown in the diagram, Fig. 44. Normally these springs tend to bring the control stick back to a central position, in which the elevator lies flat, but if one of the springs is tensioned by winding up the winch in a clockwise direction, the position to which the stick will tend to come when released will be such as to set the elevator at a positive angle. This winch gear, which is illustrated in Fig. 45, is mounted on the right-hand side of the nacelle and is therefore under the command of the pilot's companion.

The crank is furnished with a locking pawl, which engages with a ring of small holes bored in the plate of the winch. The steel springs used in conjunction with this apparatus are some 3' long and about ¾" in diameter. The inscription behind the winch reads:—

    Nose heavy—Right wind.
    Tail heavy—Left wind.

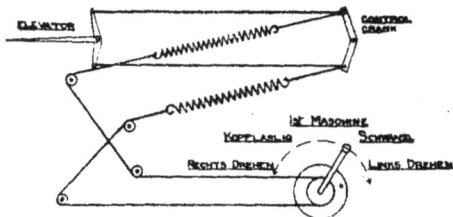

Fig. 44.

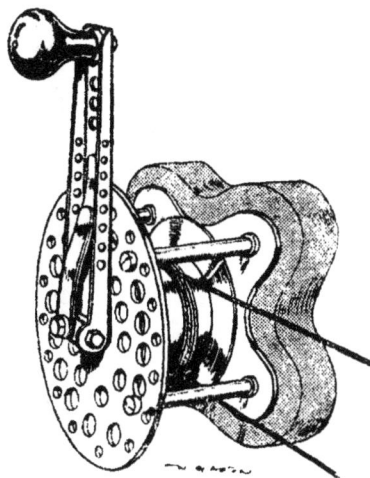

Fig. 45.

LANDING GEAR.

As might be expected, the landing gear on this machine is of massive proportions. Two vertical streamline section wood-filled tubes descend from the centre section wing spars, immediately under the engine, to a bridge piece or hollow girder made of welded steel. This is shown in the photograph Fig. 46. Through an oval hole in this girder a short axle carries two 965 mms. × 150 mms. wheels (38" × 6"). These work up and down against the tension of a bundle of steel springs about ¼" in diameter and made of wire approximately ⅟₁₆" thick. The steel girder is extensively pierced for lightness, and the edges of the holes are swaged inwards. The axle is prevented from moving sideways by plates, and is provided with short steel cables which act as radius rods and connect it to the front of the girder. The whole of the box girder is covered in with a detachable bag of fabric, which extends up to the small cross bar mounted immediately above the girder.

Mudguards are provided behind each landing wheel for the purpose of preventing any mud or stones dislodged by the wheels from coming in contact with the propellers.

From the front and rear of the box girder streamline tubes are taken to the ends of the main wing spars, where they abut against the nacelle, and these diagonals are further braced with streamline steel tubes. Both the vertical and diagonal tubes are held in split sockets so as to be easily replaceable if damaged.

In addition to the four main landing wheels, a fifth is mounted under the nose of the fuselage, as shown in the photograph Fig. 47. This wheel is 760 mms. × 100 mms (30" × 4"). It is mounted on a short tubular axle, which is capable of sliding up and down slots in its forks against a strong coil spring, and it is also capable of a certain amount of lateral movement along its axle, also against the action of two small coil springs.

The tail portion of the fuselage is protected by a fixed skid made of wood but shod with a steel sole. This is arranged, as shown in photograph Fig. 48, and is fitted with a small coil spring contained inside the fuselage.

WIRING.

The whole of the wiring system on the machine is very neatly carried out. There are three main systems; firstly, the ignition wiring, which is contained for the most part in tubes of glazed and woven fabric, secondly, the heating system, for which the wires are carried in flexible metal conduits, and thirdly, the lighting system, in which a thin celluloid protective tubing is used. Wires are run from the nacelle along the leading edge of the upper planes to points level with the outermost strut. Here they terminate in a plug fitting placed behind a hinged panel. Apparently lamps are intended to be served by this circuit. Immediately in front of the pilot's seat a universally jointed lamp bracket is mounted on the outside of the nacelle. The exact purpose of this lamp is not known, as it could not illuminate any instruments.

FIG. 47.   LANDING WHEEL UNDER THE FRONT PORTION OF THE NACELLE.

FIG. 48.   TAIL-SKID.

FIG. 49. MACHINE GUN MOUNTING IN THE FRONT PORTION OF THE
NACELLE.

FIG. 54. VIEW OF BOMB-RACK IN NACELLE. BEHIND IT CAN BE SEEN THE SPRING OF
TRIMMING GEAR.

ARMAMENT.

Both the forward and rear cockpits are furnished with swivel gun mounts carrying Parabellum machine guns. These mounts consist of built-up laminated wood turntables working on small rollers, and carry a U-shaped tubular arm for elevation. This arm is hinged to a plunger rod working through a cross head, and arranged so that the arm is normally pulled down flat on the turntable by a coil spring. The plunger can be locked in any of a series of positions by means of a bolt operated by a hand-lever through a Bowden wire. A second lever allows the turntable to be locked at any desired point. A perforated sheet-metal shield protects the cross head and spring. Small shoulder pads are fixed on the turntables; of which that in the forward cockpit has a diameter of 2' 10½", whilst in the rear the diameter is 3' 0½".

A photograph of the forward gun mounting is given in Fig. 49.

The after-gunner is prevented from damaging the propellers by two wire netting screens supported by tubular steel brackets, placed on either side of his cockpit. These are sketched in Fig. 50.

FIG. 50.

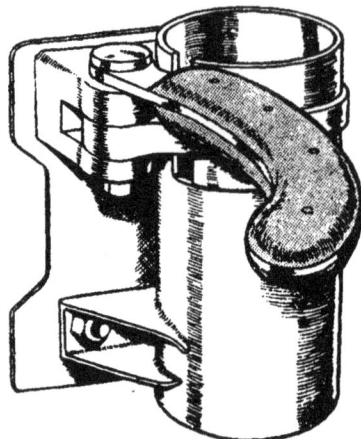

FIG. 51.

In addition to these two guns, provision is made for mounting a third in front of, and to the right of, the pilot's cockpit, where it could be managed by his companion. For this purpose a clip is provided immediately under the coaming of the nacelle, and the handle of this protrudes through a slot in the dashboard. The clip works on the eccentric principle, and appears to be self-locking. Its construction is shown in detail in Fig. 51.

A rack for Verey lights is mounted on the outside of the nacelle convenient to the pilot's companion.

INSTRUMENTS.

AIRSPEED INDICATOR.

Considerable interest attaches to the fact that this Friedrichshafen Bomber is the first enemy machine brought down which has been found provided with an airspeed indicator. This is of the static type, embodying a Pitot head of the usual type. The indicator has a dial of large size, and is altogether a much more bulky instrument than any of a similar purpose used on British machines. An investigation of its mechanism is being made.

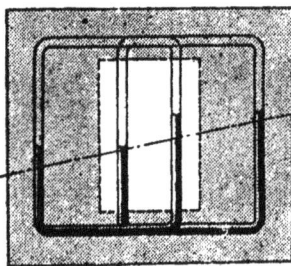

FIG. 52.

ALTIMETER.

This is of the usual type, reading to 8 kilometres.

LEVEL INDICATOR.

This is a somewhat crudely made device, employing two liquid levels, as indicated in the diagrammatic sketch Fig. 52. It will be seen that the reading gives the pilot an exaggerated idea of the angle of roll. The glass tubes are sealed up, and contain a dark blue liquid. One side of the dial is engraved Hängt links (Hangs left), the other Hängt rechts (Hangs right). The manufacturer is Arno Weisse, Berlin.

REVOLUTION COUNTERS.

The dials give readings from 300 to 1,600 r.p.m. The sector between 1,300 and 1,500 is painted black, and these figures are marked with luminous compound, as also is the indicating hand. The manufacturer is Wilhelm Morell, Leipsig.

AIR PRESSURE GAUGES.

These read from 0 to 0.5 kilogrammes per square centimetre. There is a red mark against the figure 0.25 kg. The manufacturer is Maximall Apparate Fabrik, Berlin.

ELECTRIC THERMOMETER DIAL.

This dashboard instrument consists of a box-type meter, the dial reading from 0 to 100° C. The figures 0 and 75 are accentuated by red marks. A switch at the side of the box, having positions marked 1 and 2, allows the temperature of either radiator to be read.

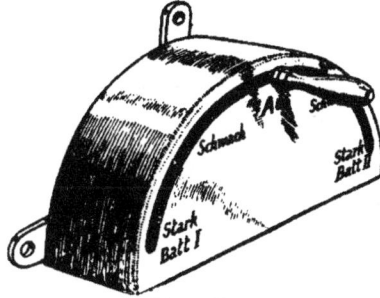

FIG. 53.

PETROL LEVEL INDICATORS.

These are of the Maximall type, and employs a float immersed in a tubular guide in the tank. This float communicates its motion to a finger working over a circular dial, by means of a thin cord passing over pulleys. These are encased in pipes which are under the same pressure as the tank.

ELECTRIC HEATING RHEOSTAT.

This is illustrated in Fig. 53. It is marked Aus (off), Schwach (weak), Stark (strong). There are two separate resistance coils, enabling the rheostat also to perform the function of a change-over switch.

WIRELESS.

The machine is internally wired for wireless, and the left-hand engine is provided with a pulley and clutch for driving the dynamo. Reference to Fig. 26 will show that this is designed to be mounted on a bracket carried by the outside front engine bearer strut, and that the engine fairing is moulded to receive it.

BOMBS AND BOMB GEAR.

At each side of the covered-in passage way in the nacelle are bomb racks, shown in Fig. 54, capable of holding five 25-pounder (12 kg.) bombs. Underneath the nacelle are carried two large tubular frames, fitted with cradles of steel cable and furnished with the usual form of trip gear. These racks, illustrated in Fig. 55, would, it is believed, be capable of supporting a 300 kg. bomb a-piece. The bombs carried, however, evidently vary with the radius of action over which the aeroplane has to operate. The large racks are not permanently attached to the nacelle, but can easily be removed as required.

Fig. 23 shows the inside of the front cockpit from which the release of the bombs is conducted. There are seven triggers for the small bomb racks and two levers for the large bomb trips, as shown in Fig. 56. The cables for this gear are carried under the floor, and are painted different colours for distinction.

BOMB SIGHT.

The bomb sight carried on the machine presents no new features, and is of the ordinary German non-precision type.

FABRIC AND DOPE.

Two entirely different kinds of fabric are employed in the Friedrichshafen machine. The wings are covered with a low-grade linen of the class which is employed on most of the enemy machines. It is white in colour. Compared with that of British fabrics, the tensile strength is fairly good.

This fabric is covered with a cellulose acetate dope, and is camouflaged in large irregular lozenges of dull colours, including blue-black, dark green, and earth colour.

The other fabric, which is applied to the fuselage, tail planes, rudder, elevator, fin and landing gear, is apparently a cheap material much inferior to British fabrics designed for a similar purpose. This fuselage fabric is dyed in a regular pattern of lozenges, the colours being hardly distinguishable from black. The dope is acetate of cellulose.

In both cases the dope seems to be carelessly applied.

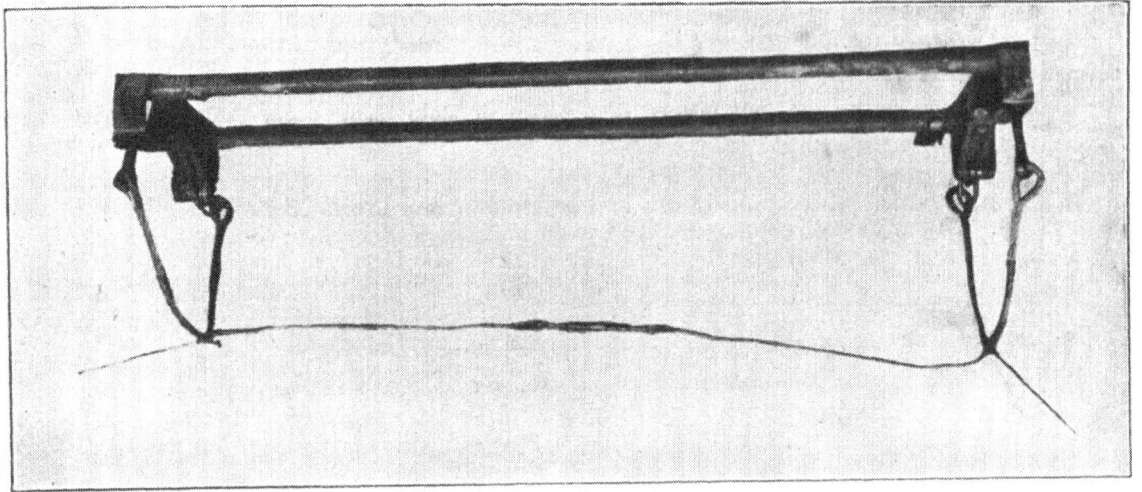

FIG. 55.   LARGE BOMB-CARRIER.

FIG. 56.   BOMB-RELEASE GEAR INSIDE FRONT COCKPIT.

22

CHANGES IN DESIGN.

When compared with the Fdh. GIII., No. 177/17 (of 13/9/17), brought down by the French, this Friedrichshafen presents a few differences in detail design, amongst which the following points may be noted :—

(1) Engine fairing. In No. 177 spinners were mounted on the propeller bosses, and an aluminium ring of large diameter mounted on the rear extremities of the engine bearers in order to carry the rearmost fairing panels.

(2) Exhaust pipe. In the No. 177 this was, as in the present case, trumpet shaped and turned back at the end, but instead of a series of slots being used, the open vent was "bottled" so that the orifice was slightly restricted, and an additional circle of small holes provided.

(3) Engine bearers. These were of ash in the No. 575, and the L-shaped extension was not used. The method of building up the bearers was, however, similar to that described.

(4) The weight empty was 2,665 kg. in the No. 177, as against 2,695 in the machine under review.

(5) The air-scoops under the engine fairing were smaller.

(6) The arrangement of the instruments, taps, etc., on the dashboard was quite different.

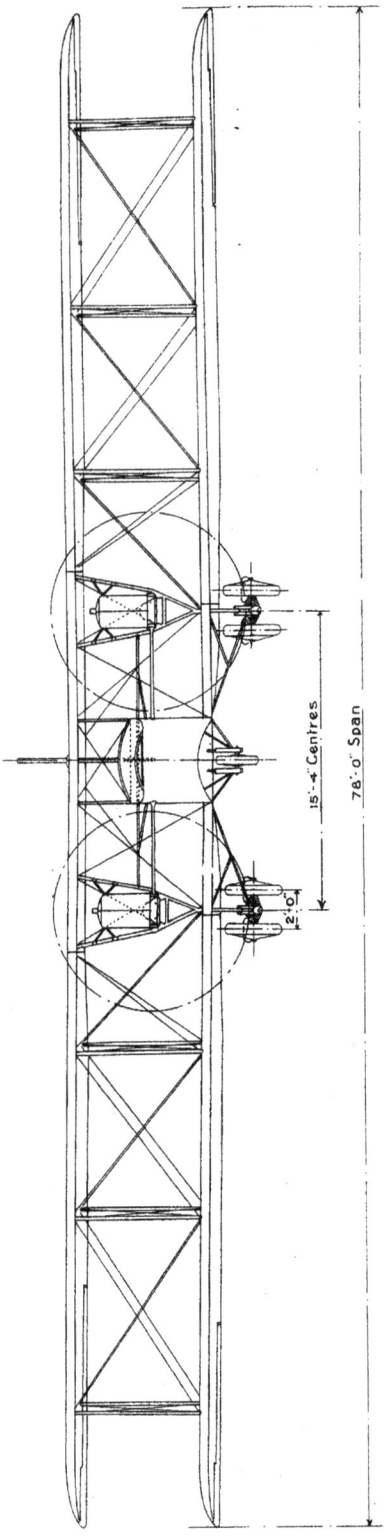

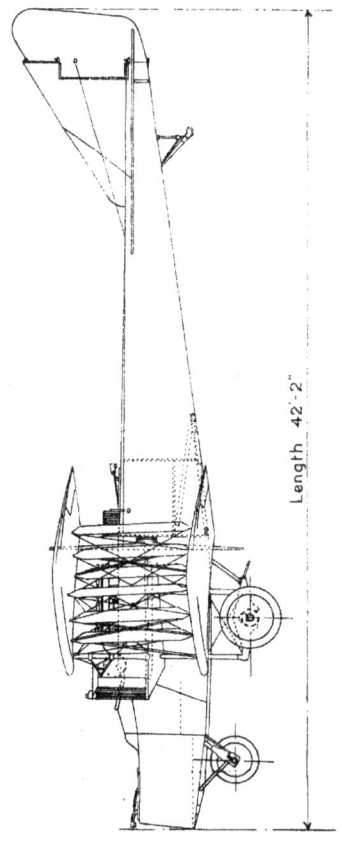

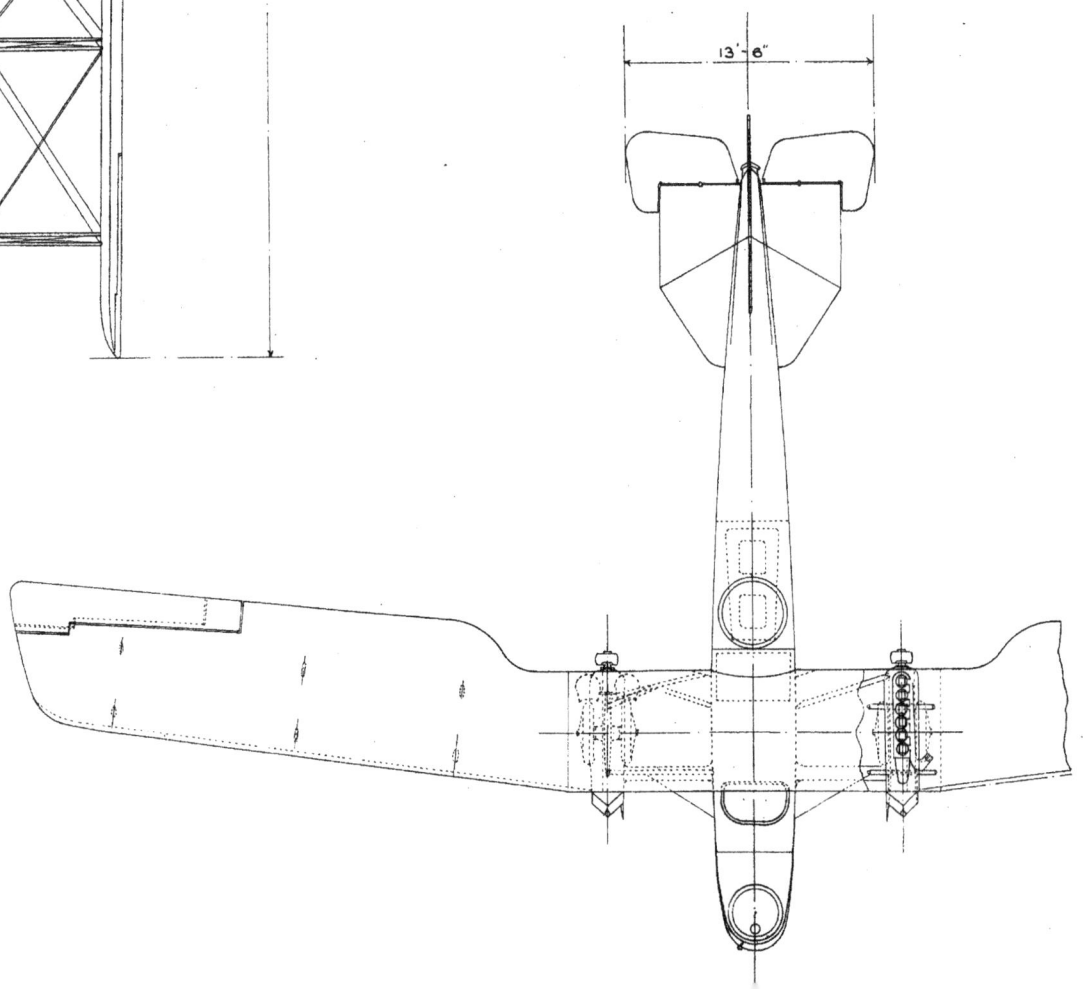

www.ingramcontent.com/pod-product-compliance
Lightning Source LLC
Chambersburg PA
CBHW081543090426
42741CB00014BA/3250